STEM IN CURRENT EVENTS

► Agriculture ► Energy ► Entertainment Industry ► Environment & Sustainability
► Forensics ► Information Technology ▼ **Medicine and Health Care**
► Space Science ► Transportation ► War and the Military

MEDICINE AND HEALTH CARE

▶ Dr. Drone?

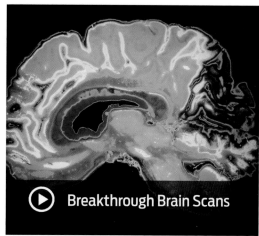

▶ Breakthrough Brain Scans

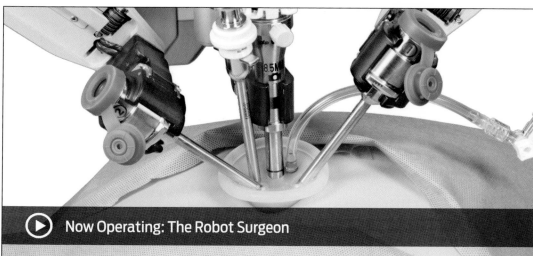

▶ Now Operating: The Robot Surgeon

Agriculture

Energy

Entertainment Industry

Environment & Sustainability

Forensics

Information Technology

Medicine and Health Care

Space Science

Transportation

War and the Military

STEM IN CURRENT EVENTS

MEDICINE AND HEALTH CARE

By Michael Burgan

MASON CREST

Mason Crest
450 Parkway Drive, Suite D
Broomall, PA 19008
www.masoncrest.com

© 2017 by Mason Crest, an imprint of National Highlights, Inc.

Printed and bound in the United States of America.

First printing
9 8 7 6 5 4 3 2 1

Series ISBN: 978-1-4222-3587-4
ISBN: 978-1-4222-3594-2
ebook ISBN: 978-1-4222-8295-3

Produced by Shoreline Publishing Group
Designer: Tom Carling, Carling Design Inc.
Production: Sandy Gordon
www.shorelinepublishing.com

Front cover: Dreamstime.com: Alexlmx tl; Katie Nesling tr. Intuitive Surgical b.

Library of Congress Cataloging-in-Publication Data

Names: Burgan, Michael.
Title: Medicine and health care / by Michael Burgan.
Description: Broomall, PA : Mason Crest, [2017] |
Series: STEM in current   events | Includes index.
Identifiers: LCCN 2016004739| ISBN 9781422235942 (hardback) | ISBN   9781422235874 (series) |
    ISBN 9781422282953 (ebook)
Subjects: LCSH: Medicine--Juvenile literature. | Medical care--Juvenile   literature.
Classification: LCC R130.5 .B85 2017 | DDC 616.07--dc23
LC record available at http://lccn.loc.gov/2016004739

Contents

Key Icons to Look For

Words to Understand: These words with their easy-to-understand definitions will increase the reader's understanding of the text, while building vocabulary skills.

Sidebars: This boxed material within the main text allows readers to build knowledge, gain insights, explore possibilities, and broaden their perspectives by weaving together additional information to provide realistic and holistic perspectives.

Educational Videos: Readers can view videos by scanning our QR codes, providing them with additional educational content to supplement the text. Examples include news coverage, moments in history, speeches, iconic sports moments, and much more!

Text-Dependent Questions: These questions send the reader back to the text for more careful attention to the evidence presented here.

Research Projects: Readers are pointed toward areas of further inquiry connected to each chapter. Suggestions are provided for projects that encourage deeper research and analysis.

Series Glossary of Key Terms: This back-of-the-book glossary contains terminology used throughout this series. Words found here increase the reader's ability to read and comprehend higher-level books and articles in this field.

INTRODUCTION
Marvels of Medicine

For thousands of years, people around the world have fought to combat the outbreak of disease and promote good health. In ancient times, some cultures thought disease was the result of evil spirits, and they turned to religion, not science, in search of cures. People called shamans were both spiritual leaders and healers. Early doctors in such places as Egypt and China also discovered that certain herbs could cure some diseases, and scientists still study the power of some plants and herbs to prevent or treat diseases. Later, the Islamic countries of the Middle East created the first large hospitals, which also trained doctors. Islamic books on surgery and other medical practices were used for several hundred years across parts of Europe, North Africa, and Asia.

Over the last 500 years, the rise of modern science has led to a greater understanding of what causes many illnesses and how they can be treated. The microscope was an important tool for studying the human body, which led to the understanding that it and all other living things are made up of cells. Some illnesses, such as cancer, start with changes that occur at the cellular level. The microscope also led to the discovery of microorganisms, such as bacteria and viruses. Scientists learned that they play a role in causing many diseases. With the "germ theory" of disease, doctors saw that good hygiene could prevent disease, and that drugs that killed a particular microorganism could cure some illnesses. Late in the 19th century, a new piece of medical technology appeared: the X-ray. For the first time, doctors could see inside the body of a living patient to diagnose illnesses or detect broken bones.

One of the greatest medical breakthroughs was the use of vaccines to prevent illness. Patients receive small doses of the virus that causes a disease. It stimulates the body's own defenses. If the actual virus enters the body afterward, the patients are able to fight off the disease. An early kind of vaccination process, called variolation, was used to prevent smallpox. The late 19th and early 20th centuries saw scientists create a number of new vaccines that saved millions of lives.

Scientists of the 20th century made another great discovery—the role of genes in shaping how living organisms reproduce and develop certain traits. Genes are made up of a combination of chemicals that form molecules called DNA. The DNA makes copies of itself that go into new cells. During the 1970s, scientists perfected genetic engineering—adding DNA from one organism into the DNA of another. The modified organism acquired some trait from the original organism. For medicine, genetic engineering led to using plants and animals to create new drugs. The study of genes also showed that harmful changes in an organism's DNA could lead to disease.

Today, trained specialists in the different branches of science, technology, engineering, and mathematics (STEM) draw on the discoveries of the past to find new ways to treat and prevent illness. Some conduct basic research into which microorganisms cause disease—and the role helpful bacteria can play in medicine. Others explore the role our genes play in keeping us well or making us sick. Technological advancements include

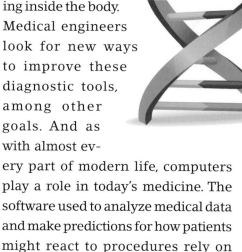

new, effective ways to deliver medicines or artificial body parts that can replace natural ones that fail. Since the X-ray, doctors have come to rely on even more precise methods for seeing inside the body. Medical engineers look for new ways to improve these diagnostic tools, among other goals. And as with almost every part of modern life, computers play a role in today's medicine. The software used to analyze medical data and make predictions for how patients might react to procedures rely on mathematics.

The advancements in medicine in just the last 50 years would stun a scientist from the past. The increase in basic knowledge about the body's workings has led to new treatments for all sorts of disease. But the quest for new knowledge and practical solutions to medical problems never ends. Today's experts in the medical STEM fields are working hard to continue to improve the world's health.

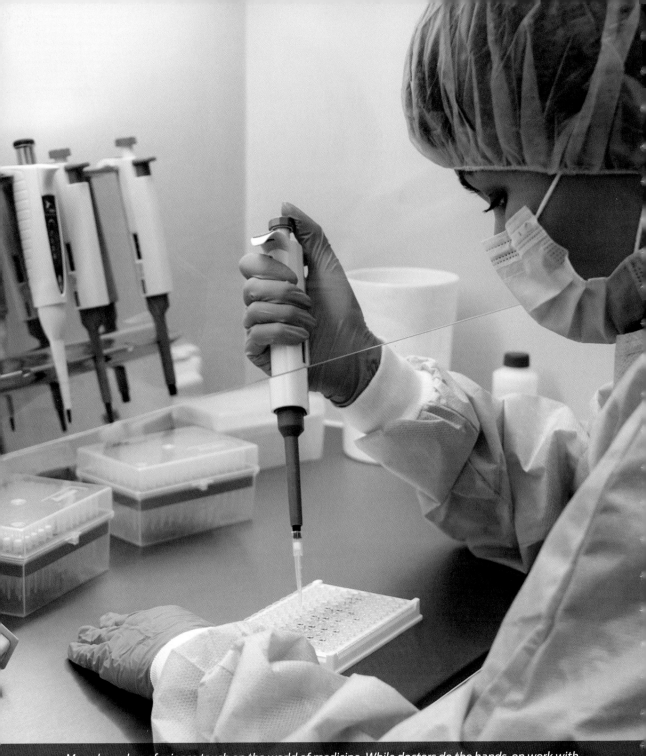

Many branches of science touch on the world of medicine. While doctors do the hands-on work with patients, research chemists study the body and its chemistry to find new cures and treatments.

SCIENCE AND
Medicine

1

Words to Understand

compound   a mixture of different elements

cultured   grew in special material in a laboratory

enzymes   types of proteins produced in cells that trigger a biological function

graft   to join living tissue from one organism to another

immune system   various cells, tissues, and organs that work together to keep the body healthy

oncologist   a doctor who specializes in treating cancer

Medical scientists usually have a background in biology or chemistry. They often specialize in one particular field within those broad categories. Neurochemists, for example, focus on the chemicals that affect how the brain operates. The larger field of biochemistry looks at the chemicals that operate throughout the entire body—various **enzymes** and other chemicals play a role in keeping the body healthy. Some medical scientists specialize in the study of genes and their role in medicine. Another area of research is immunology—the study of the **immune system**.

The Importance of Proteins

People often talk about the protein in the food they eat. They want to make sure they get enough protein to stay healthy. Humans also produce a large number of proteins in their body that play a huge role in keeping us alive. Found in cells, proteins are made up of smaller chemical substances called amino acids. Enzymes are one type of protein. One of their roles is to break down food so the body can use the nutrients it contains. Another protein is collagen, which connects and holds together bone, muscles, and other parts of the body. Antibodies are proteins that protect the body from foreign "invaders," such as bacteria and viruses.

A closer look at how proteins help the human body

Scientists want to know how the body fights off diseases and what prevents some people from doing so. The research done in the basic sciences can lead to further work that results in new treatments of specific diseases. Some scientists also study plants and animals. Plants may contain substances that prevent or treat diseases. And the health of animals, particularly mammals, can provide knowledge that offers clues for human health issues.

Help From Elephants

Even with great advancements in diagnosis and treatment, cancer remains a major health issue. Each year in the United States, about 500,000 people die from one of the many forms of the disease. Cancer occurs when cells in the body grow and divide faster than they should. Changes in genes, called mutations, lead to damage that makes cells become cancerous. In some cases, other genes can stop the growth of cancer cells or kill them completely. But if a body can't control the cancer cells, they spread and cause disease.

In recent years, a group of scientists in Utah have looked at elephants and their genes to try to understand cancer in humans. Elephants have many more cells than people and so should be at a higher risk for having some of those cells turn cancerous. That, in turn, would increase their risk of dying of the disease. But death rates from cancer for the huge mammals are actually much lower than in humans. A study released in 2015 said the answer seems to lie in certain elephant genes.

Humans have two genes that produce a protein called p53. This protein can stop the development of cancerous cells or cause the

Can elephants cure cancer? Some scientists think that these amazing animals might hold the secret to new cancer treatments in their blood.

This elephant is enjoying a treat provided by a zookeeper. But nature has given elephants a treat by providing a special gene that resists many cancers.

cell to kill itself, a process called apoptosis. Elephants, the study showed, have at least 40 copies of the gene that produces p53. Most of these copies developed over time as elephants evolved as a species. Being able to produce more p53 seems to make elephants naturally more able than humans to fight off cancer.

Joshua Schiffman, an **oncologist** who took part in the study, said that elephants would perhaps be extinct if they didn't have the ability to make cancer cells die before they spread. "Nature has already figured out how to prevent cancer," Schiffman said, thanks to p53. "It's up to us to learn how different animals tackle the problem so we can adapt those strategies to prevent cancer in people."

The study may also benefit elephants. Eric Peterson, from the Hogle Zoo in Salt Lake City, also took part in the research. He thinks that since scientists might be able to learn about cancer from elephants, people will try harder to preserve them in the wild.

A Helpful Herb

Many people enjoy seasoning their pizza or favorite pasta dish with oregano. The herb has been used for thousands of years in cooking and in medicine. Medical studies have shown that the

Is this pizza going to help you feel better? Well, the pizza might not, but the oregano being added to the sauce has been shown to have anti-inflammatory qualities.

Oil of oregano:
nature's antibiotic

oils that help give oregano its flavor can kill certain harmful bacteria. One chemical is also thought to be helpful in reducing inflammation in the body, which is associated with a number of diseases. More recently, scientists have studied what role oregano can play in fighting cancer.

The key part of oregano in the battle against cancer may be a **compound** called carvacrol. Supriya Bavadekar, a professor at Long Island University, showed that carvacrol triggers apoptosis in prostate cancer cells. A research team in the United Arab Emirates found that carvacrol has the same effect on some breast cancer cells. The oregano compound also seems to be able to stop the spread of a kind of breast cancer once it has already appeared in a woman's body.

Apart from possibly preventing the spread of some cancers, carvacrol also seems to be a potent weapon in fighting a germ called notovirus. Found in food, the virus can cause vomiting. Together with other substances that kill microorganisms, the oregano oil can kill the notovirus. Carvacrol could someday be used in cleaners to reduce the spread of disease in hospitals and other public places.

Making Medicine Easier to Take

Some of the world's volcanic hot springs are home to a microorganism called *Sulfolobus islandicus* (*S. islandicus*). It thrives in temperatures above 160°F (71°C) and in acidic conditions.

The secret to helping people take some medicines as a pill might lie in these steamy geothermal vents in Iceland, home of a very hardy microorganism.

S. islandicus is related to other microorganisms that live in some of the most extreme conditions on Earth. Being able to survive extreme heat and strong acids may make *S. islandicus* a perfect source for material to make new drug capsules.

People with certain medical conditions, such as diabetes, must take medicine daily, but it's usually only available as a liquid that must be injected. It would be easier for the patients if they could take the medicine as a pill. Some current pills, however, can't survive the stomach's strong acids to reach the small intestine, where the medicine is absorbed. Sara Munk Jensen at the University of South Denmark thinks lipids, or fats, found in *S. islandicus* hold the key for creating a capsule that can survive the journey through a person's gut.

Jensen and her team used the lipids from the microorganism to create a fatty capsule called a liposome. They added dye to the capsule and then placed it in a solution that had the same level of acid as a human stomach. To be effective, a capsule or tablet containing medicine must be able to remain intact for 90 minutes in the stomach. In the test, Jensen found that some of the liposome with the dye survived the acid bath. To make the test liposome, Jensen did not purify the lipids from *S. islandicus*. She believes a pure form of the lipid would make even more of the fatty capsule remain whole. Further testing will show if the *S. islandicus* lipids will create a new, easier way to deliver medicines.

Treating Concussions

Athletes of all ages in a variety of sports run the risk of suffering concussions. Also called a mild traumatic brain injury, a concussion results from a blow to the head and affects how the brain functions. Symptoms can include headache, nausea, or trouble concentrating. While concussions often occur during contact sports, they also can result from a fall or car accident.

In the past, doctors usually told people who suffered a concussion to rest until their symptoms went away. But starting in 2015, John Leddy, M.D., and psychologist Barry Willer at the University of Buffalo's Concussion Management Clinic began a study to see

An onfield collision for a head ball has resulted in what might be a pair of concussions for these soccer players. Scientists are focusing more than ever on concussion effects.

what role physical activity plays in speeding the recovery from a concussion.

Early tests, Leddy said, showed that "some activity is actually necessary to promote recovery." In some of the tests, students who had suffered a concussion exercised on a treadmill while their heart rate was monitored. They exercised until they began to feel symptoms and Leddy noted their heart rate. Later, the students stopped exercising just before they reached that heart rate. The exercise at that level promoted faster recovery from the concussion than simple rest did.

Stem Cell Controversy

Scientists believe stem cell research offers great promise for medicine. But the use of a certain kind of stem cell in the lab has stirred controversy. Embryonic stem cells have the ability to develop into more than 200 other kinds of cells. They come from embryos, or the collection of cells inside a pregnant woman that potentially develop into a baby. Most embryonic stem cells come from embryos mothers choose to donate to science for research. These stem cells can be easily **cultured** in a lab, compared to adult stem cells. To first get the stem cells, however, the embryo must be destroyed. Some people with strong religious or moral beliefs think it is wrong to destroy something that has the potential to turn into a living human being. These people oppose the use of embryonic stem cell research. A breakthrough in stem cell research came in 2007, when Shinya Yamanaka found a way to alter the genes of adult stem cells. He made it so they had the same ability to develop into all other cells, just as embryonic stem cells can. Further research confirmed that the altered adult cells have the same properties as the embryonic cells.

With the 2015–16 study, Leddy and Willer hope to learn the right amount and what type of exercise speeds recovery from a concussion, since too much exercise can prevent recovery. The study involved teens between 13 and 17 years old, whether they were injured in a sport or not. The study focused on teens because they take longer to recover from concussions than adults and are more apt to suffer one. One out of four young people will experience a concussion before leaving high school. One early participant in the study was 16-year-old Julia Whipple, who suffered a concussion playing soccer. She was excited to have the chance to do some exercise while she recovered. Whipple said, "I didn't want to just go home to my bedroom and wait for the symptoms to disappear." The results of Leddy and Willer's study could lead to new guidelines for treating many concussions.

The Power of Stem Cells

While every part of the human body is made up of cells, not all these cells are created equal. A special kind of cell is the stem cell. There are actually several types of stem cells and all have the ability to make exact copies of themselves. They can also divide and then develop into cells like those found throughout the human body. Stem cells are located in different parts of the body, such as the blood, skin, brain, and heart.

For medical researchers, stem cells offer hope to treat various illnesses or repair organs. Scientists can use stem cells to create cells for a particular part of the body that has been damaged, such as a bone or muscle. Dr. Carl Gregory of Texas A&M University has taken stem cells from the bone marrow of rats and used them to create new bone tissue. By 2015, he was doing

The DNA from laboratory rats such as these is being used to investigate new treatments that can create bone grafts for use in humans.

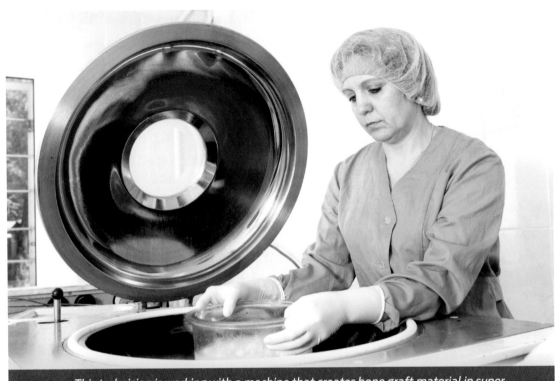

This technician is working with a machine that creates bone graft material in super-sterile conditions. Such materials can be used in operations on humans.

the same procedure on dogs. If the process works for humans, too, it could offer a better way to repair their injured bones.

Currently, doctors around the world perform more than two million bone **graft** surgeries each year. During these operations, bone tissue from one part of the patient's body or donated tissue is grafted onto damaged or diseased bones. Grafts are commonly done on hips, knees, and spine. The surgery, however, can be expensive, and the tissue is not always readily available. Creating bone tissue from the stem cells, Gregory said, "will provide a limitless supply for bone grafting."

Stem cells also play an important role in the blood stream. Blood stem cells were the first kind of stem cells discovered, during the 1960s. Blood stem cells produce all the blood cells in the body. A research team at the University of Toronto suggested that this process happens much faster than once believed, as the stem cell produces "adult" red and white blood cells. The discovery, researchers said, means better treatments for blood diseases. It also could lead to a better understanding of how some blood stem cells produce blood cells that become cancerous.

 # Text-Dependent Questions

1. How does the protein p53 affect cancer cells?

2. On average, how many children and teens will suffer a concussion before they finish high school?

3. Why do some people oppose the use of embryonic stem cells in medical research?

 # Research Project

Using the Internet, find two kinds of human proteins not mentioned in this chapter and learn what they do.

Stem cells and nutrition

Medical technology has come a long way from the simple stethoscope, in use by doctors for more than 200 years. Who knows what tech this baby might use someday?

TECHNOLOGY AND
Medicine

Words to Understand

atoms   the basic units of chemical elements

chemotherapy   a medical treatment using one or more drugs that kill cancer cells

hormone   a natural substance produced in cells that travels to different parts of the body and influences its growth and function

pathogen   something harmful that enters the body and can cause illness

tumor   a mass of cancer cells

For many years, medical technology was as simple as using a stethoscope, which doctors use to listen to a patient's heartbeat. The stethoscope was invented in 1816 by a doctor too shy to put his ear to a female patient's chest. He used rolled-up paper to amplify the sound of the woman's beating heart. Soon stethoscopes were made from wood; now, they are made with metal and rubber.

Technology has created a host of medical devices, such as this ultrasound machine that gives an accurate real-time image of a fetus inside a mother.

Today, medical technology often relies on electronics and computers to perform a variety of tasks. These devices can record the rhythm of heartbeats, measure brain waves, deliver drugs, and help in diagnosing diseases. Technology research of today and tomorrow will keep looking for better ways to find diseases, perform surgery, and measure patients' progress as they grapple with their medical conditions.

Wearable Technology

Since 2008, anyone has been able to buy a piece of wearable technology to track their exercise habits. One of these devices, the FitBit, lets wearers know how far they walk and how many calories they burn, among other health statistics. The device's popularity squares with what many doctors have found: patients like the ease of using wearable medical technology.

Devices that doctors commonly prescribe include glucose monitors and insulin pumps for people with diabetes. Glucose is a type of sugar found in the body, and people with diabetes watch their levels of it to make sure it doesn't get too high or too low. Too much glucose can damage the body. Too little can make a person pass out or have a seizure. Wearable glucose monitors have a small patch with a wire that goes under the skin and checks

Medical tech is going mainstream. The growth in popularity of wearable tech devices has led to developments such as the FitBit, designed to help people monitor their activity.

the glucose in the patient's blood. The device then transmits the data to a separate monitor in the pocket that shows the sugar levels. These measurements occur every five minutes. Doctors can download up to three months of the numbers to see how they change over time.

Insulin is a **hormone** used to treat diabetes. An insulin pump continually sends insulin into the body and can alter the amount as needed. The pump is more convenient to use than injections, which were traditionally used to give patients insulin. The first pumps appeared during the 1970s, but their large size made them hard to use. Technology has improved the pumps so they are smaller and easier to use.

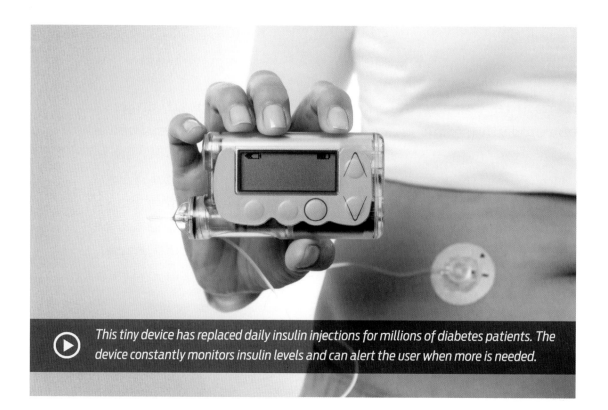

This tiny device has replaced daily insulin injections for millions of diabetes patients. The device constantly monitors insulin levels and can alert the user when more is needed.

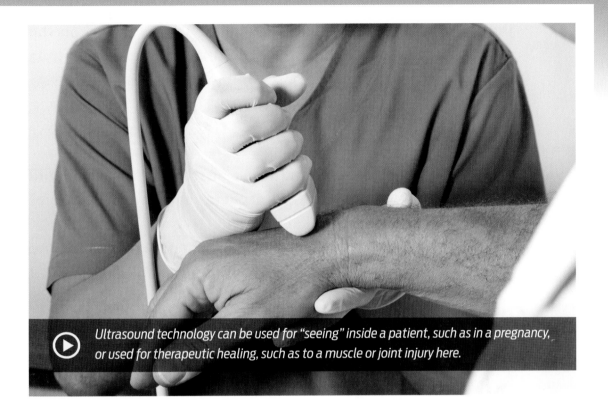

Ultrasound technology can be used for "seeing" inside a patient, such as in a pregnancy, or used for therapeutic healing, such as to a muscle or joint injury here.

A more recent wearable medical device is a small, battery-powered ultrasound device. Ultrasound is a level of sound waves too high for people to hear. It's often used in physical therapy to help injuries heal. A small machine called a Professional System can deliver ultrasound for up to four hours. The patient puts a patch on the injured area. The patch is connected to a device smaller than a typical cell phone, which generates the ultrasound. The U.S. government approved the device, and some patients using it reported almost immediate relief.

Stephen Huot, professor of medicine at Yale University, sees benefits in doctors who prescribe wearable technology. Some of the devices give both the doctors and patients real-time data about their medical condition. The doctors don't have to rely on the patients to keep track of data. Medical experts expect wearable technology to become even more common over the next 10 years.

Detection Devices for Inside the Body

Doctors have a range of methods of treating cancer, from **chemotherapy** to radiation, a form of energy that can kill cancer cells. But at times, doctors can't tell precisely how effective the treatments are while patients undergo them. A biopsy, or the removal of living cells from the patient, is one method, but it is invasive—it requires cutting into the patient. A new sensor promises to provide useful information without repeated invasive tests.

The sensor was developed at the Massachusetts Institute of Technology's Koch Institute for Integrative Cancer Research. Doctors implant the sensor in the patient's **tumor** when they do their initial biopsy. Then, as the cancer treatment goes on, the sensor transmits data wirelessly to a device outside the patient. The sensor measures two things that indicate if a tumor is shrinking: its acid levels and the amount of dissolved oxygen in it. Tumors that are shrinking because of chemotherapy release more acid. With radiation treatment, low levels of oxygen can indicate the tumor is not shrinking.

The importance of the sensor is clear to Michael Cima, a professor of engineering who helped develop it at the Koch Institute. "Rather than waiting months to see if the tumor is shrinking, you could get an early read to see if you're moving in the right direction." That gives doctors more time to adjust their treatments.

So far the sensors have been tested over several weeks while inside rodents. In the future, Cima believes, they could be placed in humans to monitor health over several years.

Another new sensor under development from the Koch Institute could prove useful on the battlefield or in a sports arena. The device measures temperature and heart and breathing rates after a patient swallows it. The heart and breathing rates are measured by sound, just as doctors do with a stethoscope. The sensor has a tiny microphone that can tell the difference between the sound of a beating heart and the lungs' sounds as air moves in and out. The device is about the size of a multivitamin. In tests

This device used to monitor tumors inside a person's body looks massive, but it is actually smaller than your little fingernail.

Military medical personnel, here in a field training exercise, might someday be able to read their soldiers' health levels on a monitor with info from implanted devices.

in pigs, the sensor successfully distinguished between the two sounds, even when the animals' digestive systems were making noise after the pigs ate. The information collected was sent to a receiver about 10 feet (3 m) away from the test animals.

When the device is perfected for humans, the military could use it to monitor the health of soldiers while they fight. The device could do the same for athletes while they're playing their sport. Future versions of the pill sensor might be able to detect specific heart or lung conditions, such as an irregular heartbeat or asthma.

More Detection Tech

New technology often provides doctors with fast and accurate ways to diagnose a variety of illnesses and medical conditions. European researchers working in Germany demonstrated a scanner that can detect arthritis of the hand at the disease's early stages.

The two major forms of arthritis can't be cured. But one of them in particular, rheumatoid arthritis, can by managed if it is caught early. Traditional X-rays can only detect the disease when it has worsened and might resist treatment. MRIs are more effective at early detection but are more expensive. The new scanner uses lasers and ultrasound to provide early detection at an affordable price. The device focuses on the finger joints, where signs of arthritis often first appear.

The scanner's laser pulses slightly warm the finger, causing joint tissue to expand. The ultrasound detects the amount of expansion, which indicates the amount of inflammation present. The device also emits a strong white light. Certain

Medical Magnets

Unlike the small magnets used to detect sickle cells, much larger ones are at the heart of magnetic resonance imaging (MRI). The principles behind using magnets and sound waves to make images dates to the 1930s. In 1977, the first image of a human was taken with an MRI device. The image produced is not a picture. It shows radio signals released by the body's hydrogen **atoms** after they are exposed to a magnetic field. Unlike an X-ray or CT scan, the MRI does not release radiation. MRIs are particularly useful in detecting problems in the body's soft tissue and the nervous system.

In recent years, some supporters of alternative medicine have claimed that magnets can be used to stop pain. Patients sometimes sleep on the magnets or wear them in jewelry. Scientific studies, however, show that the magnets have no real effect. People who claim to feel pain relief may be experiencing what is called the "placebo effect." At times, a person's belief that a medicine or procedure works makes them feel better, even if the medicine has no real effect.

wavelengths of light are absorbed where inflammation occurs. The scanner detects inflammation by analyzing the wavelength of the light not absorbed.

Less common than arthritis are a group of blood disorders collectively called sickle cell disease. The name refers to the shape of the affected blood cells, which are curved like a sickle, not round like normal cells. For the people who develop it, sickle cell disease poses serious health risks, including damage to vital organs and early death. Biomedical engineers from several New England universities have worked together to create a simple and cheap way to diagnose sickle cell disease and track its progress.

Sickle cell disease is inherited, so infants from certain back-grounds can be tested for the disease. It is most common among African Americans or people currently living in Africa, but it can also affect Hispanics, South Indians, and people from the Middle East or southern Europe. For young children, early testing and diagnosis is crucial for proper treatment.

With the new test, the diagnostic device is connected to a smart-phone. Blood from the patient is mixed with a solution that contains salt. The solution makes the sickle-shaped cells easier to detect. The blood then goes inside a special container that is placed inside the testing device. Using magnets and an LED light, the device determines if sickle-shaped cells are present. The magnets make those cells float out of the blood, making them easier to see. The smartphone's camera then takes a picture that shows any sickle cells that are present. The test provides results in about 15 minutes, compared to several days for existing tests for

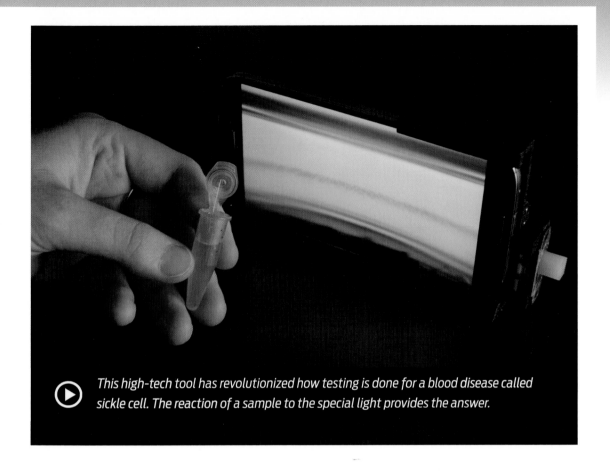

This high-tech tool has revolutionized how testing is done for a blood disease called sickle cell. The reaction of a sample to the special light provides the answer.

sickle cell disease. And unlike some older tests, the new method is easy to use in remote locations. It produces better results, too.

Using smartphones to help make medical diagnoses is not new, said Stephanie Knowlton of the University of Connecticut. She was part of the team that created the diagnostic device. But the new device uses the phones in a more advanced way. Knowlton said, "Some people have been using smartphones to look at tissue slides or blood smears. We're looking at the actual real-time activity of these cells and what they are doing in response to a magnetic field."

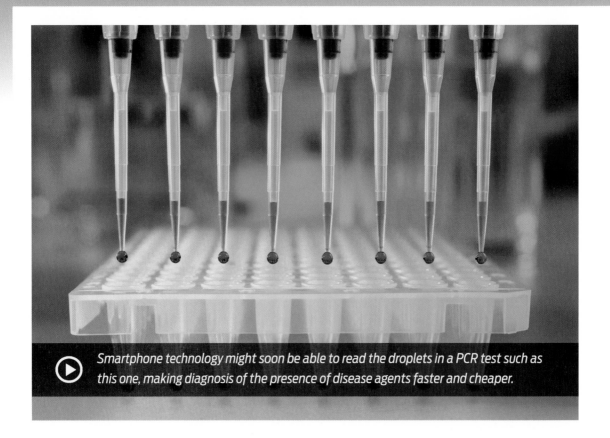

Smartphone technology might soon be able to read the droplets in a PCR test such as this one, making diagnosis of the presence of disease agents faster and cheaper.

Smartphones also play a role in another new diagnostic test, one designed to quickly detect infectious diseases. Today, doctors use a technique called polymerase chain reaction (PCR) to look for the DNA of microorganisms that might cause an infection. The PCR makes millions of copies of the DNA in about an hour or so. Even that amount of time, however, can be too long for a patient with a serious infection that requires immediate treatment.

The new diagnostic test, developed by a team at the University of Arizona, is called DOTS qPCR. It's faster, cheaper, and easier to use than the traditional PCR method of detection. It can identify a possible **pathogen** in less than four minutes. The first tests were done to look for the presence of Ebola, an often-deadly virus. A blood sample goes into a drop of water that sits in a small amount of oil. Heat from the handheld diagnostic tool triggers the reaction that makes the copies of the virus's DNA, if it's present in the sample. As more copies appear, they move toward the boundary of the oil and water and change the surface tension there. A smartphone camera measures the size of the drop and its changes, indicating if a pathogen is present. The team that created the new technique hopes it will be used in emergency rooms to detect a number of diseases and to provide both doctors and patients immediate results from a biopsy.

 Text-Dependent Questions

1. What is one benefit of wearable medical technology for patients?

2. What is one measurable sign that a tumor is shrinking after chemotherapy?

3. A smartphone and magnets are part of a system used to detect what disease?

 Research Project

Find statistics from a U.S. government agency that show the three most common forms of cancer among Americans.

•Valley Medical Building

•Main Hospital Entrance

↑ EMERGENCY

NEXT ENTRANCE

↑ EMERGENCY
NEXT ENTRANCE

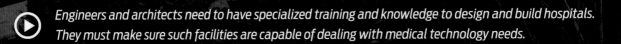

Engineers and architects need to have specialized training and knowledge to design and build hospitals. They must make sure such facilities are capable of dealing with medical technology needs.

ENGINEERING AND
Medicine

In the STEM fields, engineering is the branch that takes on construction of big things, with engineers relying on the work of scientists, computer experts, and others to help them get the job done. Medicine has fewer needs for big buildings or large devices, though they can play a part. Most medical engineers, however, work on a smaller scale. They are called biomedical engineers. They take the principles of chemistry and biology, combine them with areas such as mechanical and chemical engineering, and apply them to medical tools and techniques. Some of these tools are small, while some are large. All help make it easier for doctors to diagnose and treat disease.

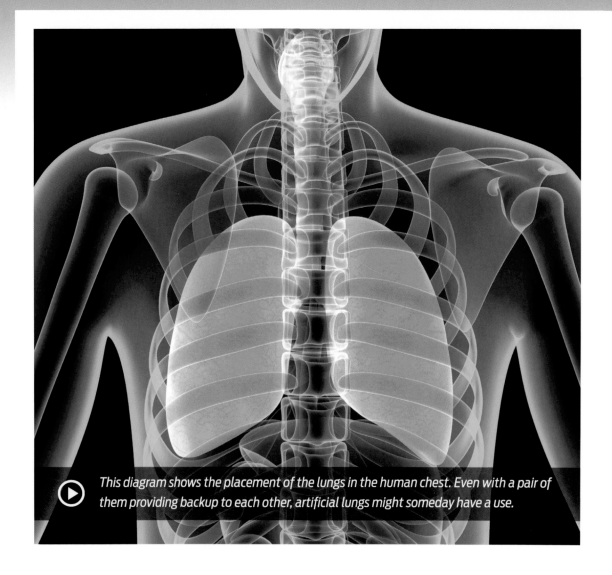

This diagram shows the placement of the lungs in the human chest. Even with a pair of them providing backup to each other, artificial lungs might someday have a use.

An Artificial Lung

How do harmful particles in the air travel through and affect the lungs? What are the best ways to deliver medicines to treat **respiratory** problems? Finding answers to those questions may now be a little easier, thanks to the development of a life-sized artificial lung. The lung was designed and tested by biomedical engineers at the Technion-Israel Institute of Technology. For the first time, researchers will have a way to study how tiny particles travel through alveolar tissue, which makes up the deepest part of the lung. The particles are usually much smaller than a grain of sand.

Closeup look at artificial lungs

Human lung tissue contains hundreds of millions of tiny pockets called air sacs. Wrapped around the sacs are tiny blood vessels called capillaries. The blood cells in the capillaries send carbon dioxide into the sacs and receive oxygen in return. The cells then carry the oxygen through the rest of the body so it can function properly.

Before the development of the new artificial lung, scientists had to use animal lungs or computer programs to study how particles in the air affected the air sacs. In some cases, they also used lungs taken from **autopsies**, but they had no way to study the functioning of the lungs in a living person. The new artificial lung moves in and out, just as human lungs do as they inhale and exhale. The lungs should help research-

Artificial Organs

In recent years, scientists have worked on creating artificial devices that can breathe for patients with lung problems or while they waited for lung transplants. One that's being tested is about the size of a soda can. Artificial organs are useful when human organs are not available for a transplant. In 1885, Max von Frey and M. Gruber built a machine that could perform the functions of the heart and lungs. Machines that serve as artificial kidneys are used for a treatment called dialysis. The first one, built in 1943, used parts from old cars and washing machines. In 1982, a totally artificial heart was put inside a patient for the first time. Almost 20 years later, doctors created an improved artificial heart still used today.

ers pinpoint how foreign particles move through the lungs' tiniest openings.

Getting a Better Look

Since the discovery of X-rays and their use in medicine, biomedical engineers and other researchers have looked for better ways to see inside the body. A method of imaging called positron emission tomography (PET) dates to the 1960s. The process involves giving

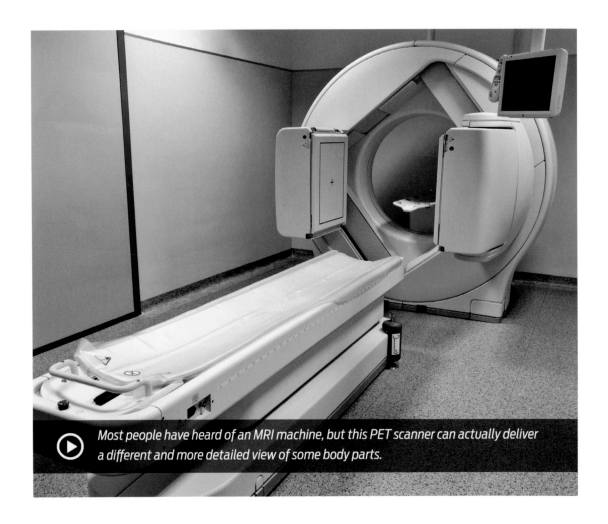

Most people have heard of an MRI machine, but this PET scanner can actually deliver a different and more detailed view of some body parts.

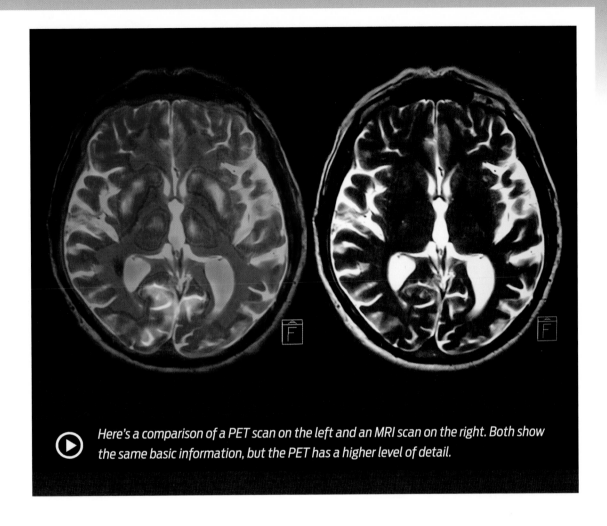

Here's a comparison of a PET scan on the left and an MRI scan on the right. Both show the same basic information, but the PET has a higher level of detail.

a patient a radioactive substance called a tracer. The tracer helps the scanner detect how a particular organ is functioning and is often used with cancer patients. A PET scan can show changes in the organ's function that indicate the beginning of a disease or how well treatments are working. Those changes would not show up on other imaging processes, such as an MRI or CT scan. The PET scans are done in segments that cover about eight inches at a time.

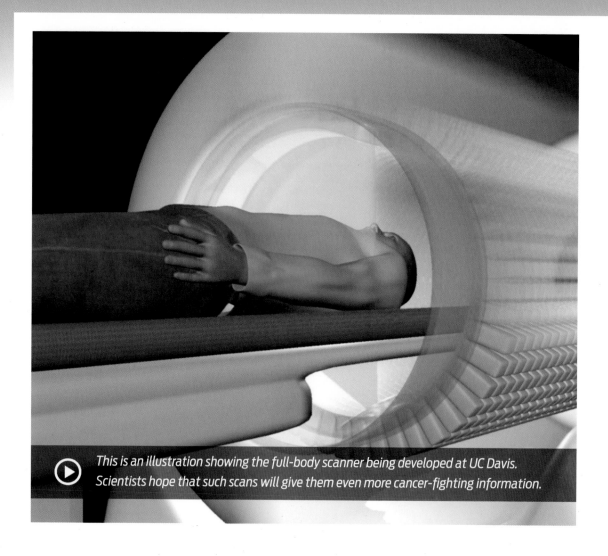

This is an illustration showing the full-body scanner being developed at UC Davis. Scientists hope that such scans will give them even more cancer-fighting information.

Researchers at the University of California, Davis, received $15.5 million from the U.S. government to build the first PET scanner that can scan a patient's entire body at once. The researchers had already been working on the design of the scanner, which will be about six feet long. The new scanner will have several advantages over the older models. Doctors will have more information about how cancer or another disease is affecting the entire body. Knowing this, they should be able to design better treatments.

The new scanner will also be faster, so patients will be exposed to less radiation. Plus, a faster scan means the images are likely to be clearer, since it will be easier for patients to remain still for a shorter period of time. The whole-body scanner should also help in the developments of new medicines. Researchers will see almost immediately how the medicine moves through the body and if it affects organs that it shouldn't.

A closeup look at making a robotic arm

Ralph de Vere White is the director of the cancer center at the university. "If this works, it's going to change medicine," he said about the full-body scanner. "It's going to change cancer detection and how we evaluate therapies."

Building Better Robotics

In common usage, some modern **prosthetic** limbs are called robotic, because they look like the arms or legs of a robot in a science fiction movie. But creating a prosthetic hand that gives a person a sense of touch is reality, not fiction.

Previously, some people given high-tech prosthetic limbs could use their thoughts to control them, sending electrical signals from a device implanted in the brain. The U.S. military backed the project because so many troops were losing limbs in battle overseas. The technology would help civilians as well. Researchers working for the U.S. government recently demonstrated an improved hand that actually gives the wearer a sense of touch.

Sensors in the fingers send signals to the brain to create the sense of touch in the robotic hand. Giving a person a sense of touch in a prosthetic hand makes the electrical process two way. The brain not only sends out signals to move the hand, but also receives signals back to help give the user more precise control.

That kind of precision is also useful for surgeons who use robotic arms during operations. The arms hold surgical tools and are controlled by the doctor with a computer. Video cameras help the doctor see inside the patient. Robotic-assisted surgeries are done to transplant organs, perform joint replacements, and

Designed by engineers and controlled in part by a patient's nerves, prosthetic hands such as this one have vastly improved in recent years.

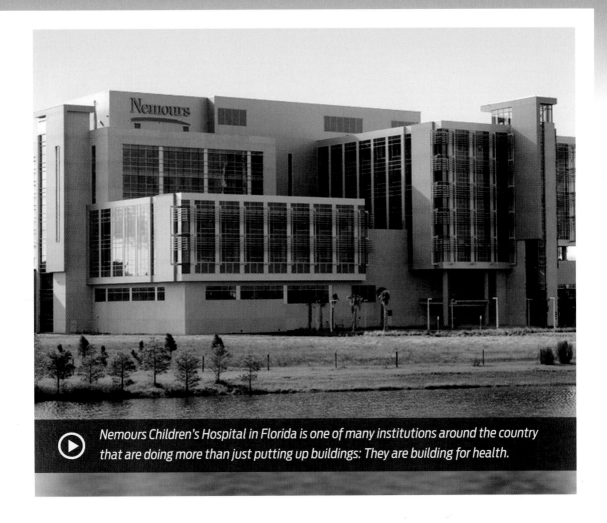

Nemours Children's Hospital in Florida is one of many institutions around the country that are doing more than just putting up buildings: They are building for health.

remove cancerous tissue. In many of the procedures, the surgeons make only tiny cuts to insert the video camera and their tools. For patients, such surgery can result in faster recovery times and less pain after the operation.

A Healing Hospital

Can a building's design affect how patients respond to treatment? For the architects and engineers who created the Nemours

The waiting rooms and check-in areas of the Nemours hospital were all designed with young patients in mind. Note the bright colors and welcoming walls.

Children's Hospital of Orlando, Florida, the answer is yes. The hospital was designed using ideas taken from several medical studies. Researchers have found that patients heal faster and need less pain medicine when their rooms face out into nature and are filled with natural sunlight. So the builders of the Nemours hospital included floor-to-ceiling windows throughout the building—natural light can fill every room. The hospital is located in a wooded area, and it has its own one-acre (0.4 ha) "discovery garden" designed to stimulate the senses of its young patients. They can smell flowers as they bloom and play art pieces that sound like drums. Two more green spaces are located on rooftops.

Since receiving medical care can be stressful for both children and their parents, the hospital was designed so that parents could easily spend the night with their kids. Patient rooms have extra beds for parents, and the hospital provides a laundry room. When their children are receiving treatment, the parents can explore the grounds or wait in lounges that overlook the greenery outside. In their free time, the kids can choose from several playrooms. Small touches include letting children choose the color lighting they want in their rooms and putting in ceilings that are not reflective. As chief medical officer Dr. Lane Donnelly explained, "When the children are in bed, they don't like to look at themselves attached to tubes and machines."

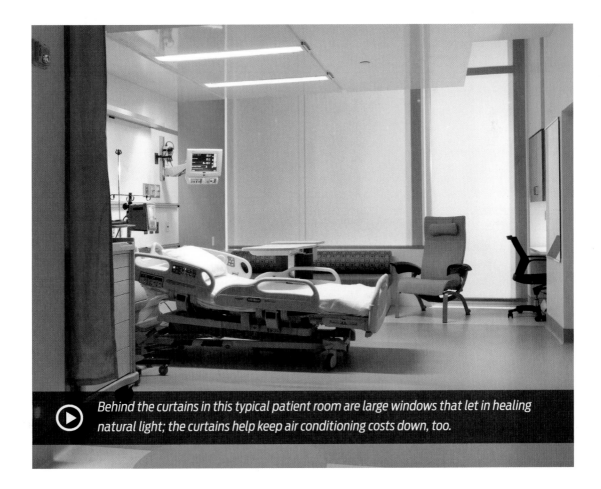

Behind the curtains in this typical patient room are large windows that let in healing natural light; the curtains help keep air conditioning costs down, too.

The builders' goal was to do as much as they could to reduce patients' stress. The architects and engineers also made the hospital a "smart" building to reduce energy and water use. Special screens on the windows reduce the amount of heat that comes in through the day, which cuts down on air conditioner use. The rooftop gardens not only provide healing green space; they also help reduce energy costs. And building materials inside the hospital are low in chemicals that can create such health problems as headaches and nausea.

This garden at a hospital in France shows how some places are working toward making the outside of their facilities as healing and positive as the treatments inside.

While newly built hospitals have an easier time being "green" to both save energy and promote healing, older hospitals have tried to add more plants and green space to their buildings. Those changes seem to help the well-being of staff and visitors as well as patients.

 ## Text-Dependent Questions

1. What is one possible benefit of the proposed whole-body PET scanner?

2. Putting patients in hospital rooms with plenty of natural light and windows that overlook green spaces can have what positive effects?

3. What do blood cells in the lung receive from the air sacs?

 ## Research Project

On the Internet, look for a research project designed to create an improved prosthetic limb. What makes the new version better than older ones?

A doctor who doesn't know math—whether for calculating test results, understanding patient statistics, or following the economics of her profession—is like a doctor without a stethoscope.

MATH AND
Medicine

Mathematics is at the heart of much of the research that goes on in science. It's also an essential part of working out engineering problems. While in everyday life we might use math to balance a checkbook or figure out the mileage our car gets, more complex math is key to medical science. Engineers use mathematical formulas to design computer software, and computers are essential to today's medical research. So, too, is the need to look for patterns in large amounts of data so people can do things more effectively. That systematic study of information is sometimes called Big Data. In various forms, math and numbers are behind important developments in medicine.

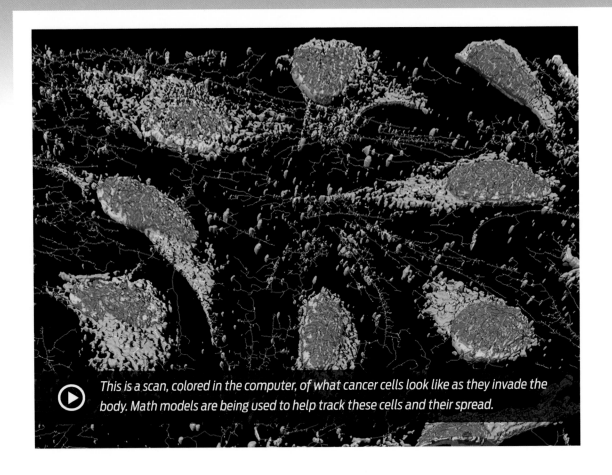

This is a scan, colored in the computer, of what cancer cells look like as they invade the body. Math models are being used to help track these cells and their spread.

Finding Where a Cancer Starts

When most patients develop cancer, doctors can pinpoint where it first started. In some cases in which cancer has spread, however, doctors know cancer is present without being able to determine its source. Knowing where a cancer started plays a role in how doctors treat it. Without that knowledge, the doctors may have to use a mixture of chemotherapy drugs, resulting in more side effects for the patient. A computer program, however, may now be able to help doctors locate the source of some cancers that previously could not be traced.

In computer science, the specific set of instructions that tell a computer what to do is called an algorithm. Scientists at the Technical University of Denmark have developed a computer program that uses algorithms to analyze mutations in the DNA of cancer cells. The program draws on information in the computer about the genetic structure of known tumors and their source. With that knowledge, the computer can look at the DNA from cancer cells that come from an unknown source and predict where they most likely came from. In tests, the program could find the source with an 85 percent chance of being correct.

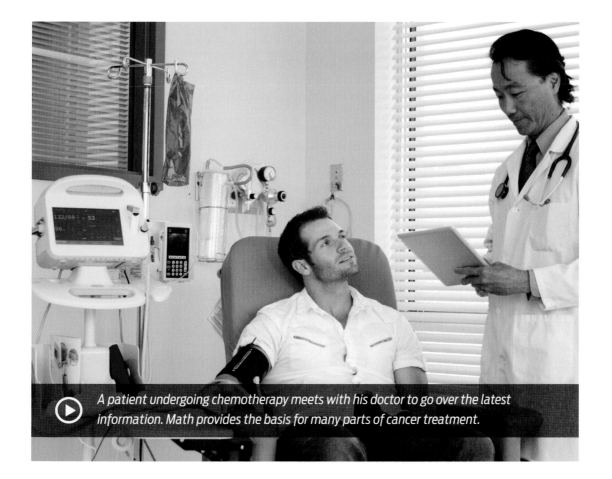

A patient undergoing chemotherapy meets with his doctor to go over the latest information. Math provides the basis for many parts of cancer treatment.

Doctors have already studied the DNA of tumors to learn if a certain cancer treatment may be more effective than another. The new computer method of detection, called Tumor Tracer, gives doctors another way to use DNA in cancer treatment. In the future, the method could also be used to diagnose cancer at its earliest stages. With some cancers, cancerous cells appear in the bloodstream before any symptoms occur. People at high risk of developing certain cancers could be screened with a test that looks for genetic evidence of cancer cells. If those cells are detected, Tumor Tracer could help doctors determine where the cancer started.

Predicting How Drugs Affect Patients

Odds are, when you've been sick you've taken some kind of medication. It might have been one you bought over the counter at the drugstore or one that was prescribed by a doctor. Medicines are made up of chemical compounds designed to target the proteins in the body that trigger your **symptoms**. Some drugs, however, interact with proteins not associated with the illness and lead to side effects. In some cases, people who take more than one medicine at the same time might find that how the drugs interact can also lead to side effects. In extreme cases, a side effect can lead to death.

One way to predict a possible side effect, or **adverse** reaction, is to study fragments of the chemicals in the drug that are easily altered. Those fragments, called labiles, can turn into molecules that will trigger a side effect. At times, though, drug companies don't uncover these fragments and their harmful side effects

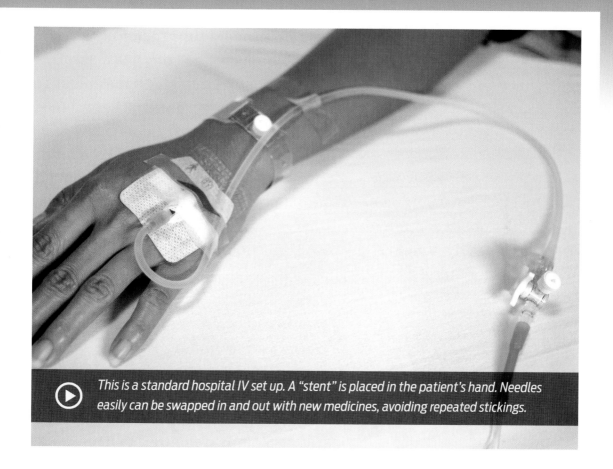

This is a standard hospital IV set up. A "stent" is placed in the patient's hand. Needles easily can be swapped in and out with new medicines, avoiding repeated stickings.

until they have already spent a lot of time and money developing the drug. In some cases, the companies might not discover the problem until after the drug is in stores. At that point, they have to remove the drug from the market.

Researchers in Spain have been working on improving the computer models that predict which drugs might produce harmful side effects. Along with information on labiles, the new method looks at data from other sources. One set of data it looks at is how similar the new drug is to existing ones. Another predicts how the drug will affect molecules and cells in the body.

The Gut-Brain Connection

One recent area of research in medicine is the possible link between microbes in the gut and the brain. Tests done with mice suggested that putting microbes from brave mice into shy ones could make the shy ones more adventurous. Other tests have suggested a link between other behaviors and conditions and the presence or absence of certain microbes. For example, the disease autism may be linked to chemicals produced by some gut bacteria. These and other microbes may change the chemistry in the brain, though researchers are not sure how. Some researchers, though, think much more work has to be done to clearly show if the gut microbes affect the brain. As researcher Rob Knight said in 2015, "It's very difficult to tell if microbial differences you see associated with diseases are causes or consequences."

The new model for predicting a drug's possible adverse reaction will make drug development safer. Medicines must go through tests with humans before they are released. The new model could point out drugs that are not worth developing and testing on humans because of the possible side effects.

Tracking Our Bacteria

Living inside and on all humans is a large number of microorganisms. Some can cause disease, while others help the body stay healthy. Together, these organisms are called the human **microbiome**, and a software program called QIIME is helping scientists around the world track the research being done on the microbiome.

QIIME—pronounced "chime"—was built by a team of computer scientists led by Rob Knight of the University of California, San Diego, School of Medicine. The software was first developed when Knight and other researchers were at the University of Colorado. Since then, they have made improvements to the software, and by 2015 it was made more readily available through a website that stores and tracks scientific data in the **cloud**.

Two major studies are currently underway to identify the microorganisms in the human microbiome and analyze their DNA. Knight and his lab are in charge of one of them, the American Gut Project, which focuses on the **microbes** in the human stomach and intestines. Volunteers send in samples from their body (not just the gut, if they choose) to Knight's lab, which analyzes the information. The data is combined with the results of other volunteers. People who take part also fill out a questionnaire about such things as their diet and lifestyle. One goal of the project is to understand how those factors determine who has what microorganisms in their gut.

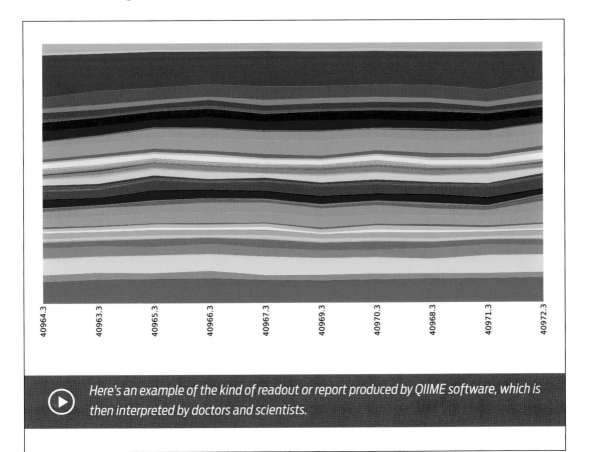

Here's an example of the kind of readout or report produced by QIIME software, which is then interpreted by doctors and scientists.

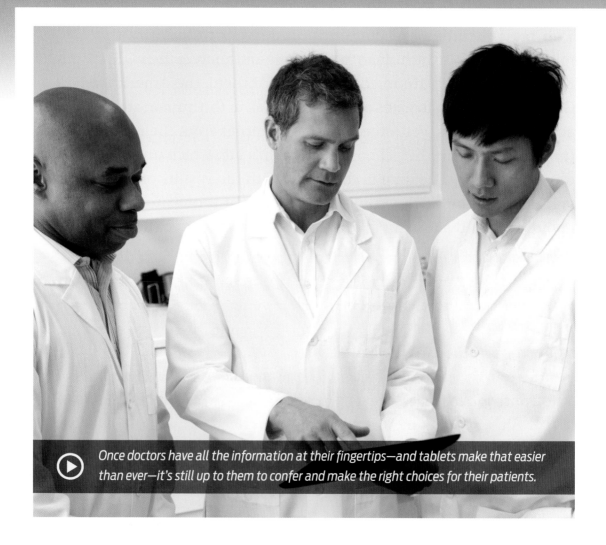

Once doctors have all the information at their fingertips—and tablets make that easier than ever—it's still up to them to confer and make the right choices for their patients.

With QIIME, information gathered in this and other research projects makes it easier for scientists to share their data. Larry Smarr, another professor at UC San Diego, says the data on QIIME will help him see the differences in the microbiome of a healthy person compared to someone who has irritable bowel disease. That knowledge could lead to treatments for the disease and tests for predicting who might develop it.

Big Data and Medicine

What could be one of the biggest breakthroughs in medicine? Using Big Data to find new cures. Researchers create huge amounts of information in a particular field. Now, computers and special algorithms allow medical scientists to combine that data and look for patterns that can help treat diseases.

In one study done at Stanford University, researchers led by Atul Butte looked at information from two different sets of public data. One set shows how certain diseases affect a patient's cells. The other looked at how certain medicines affect cells. Combined, the two sets of data showed patterns that could suggest that a medicine designed to treat one disease might be useful in treating another. One actual example: Butte and his team saw that a drug approved to treat depression might also treat a form of lung cancer. Since the medicine was already approved for human use, it would not have to go through the same lengthy testing process a new drug would.

Another use of Big Data is tracking the spread of deadly diseases, such as Ebola. That happened in 2014, when Ebola killed several thousand people in Africa. The U.S. Centers for Disease Control (CDC) worked with a software company to map where people who called a medical help line were located. Most people used cell phones, making their location easy to track. With the call information, the CDC could see if many calls were coming from a particular area. That could indicate that the Ebola virus was spreading in that region, and health workers could be sent there.

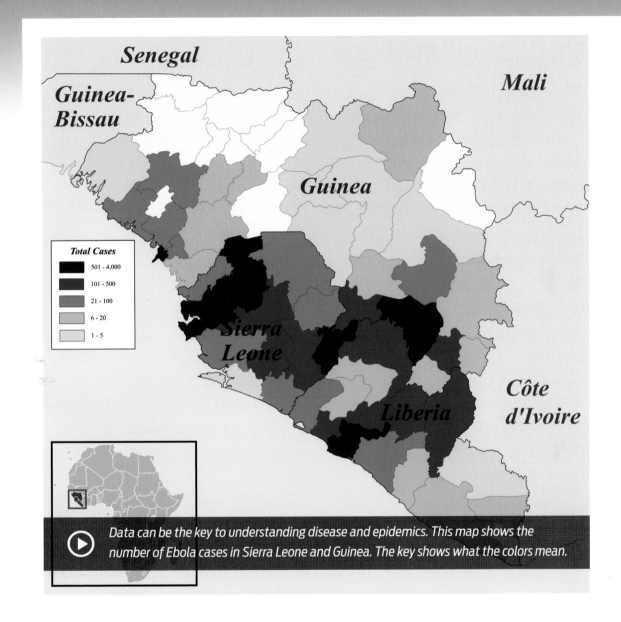

Total Cases

| 501 - 4,000 |
| 101 - 500 |
| 21 - 100 |
| 6 - 20 |
| 1 - 5 |

Senegal

Guinea-Bissau

Mali

Guinea

Sierra Leone

Liberia

Côte d'Ivoire

Data can be the key to understanding disease and epidemics. This map shows the number of Ebola cases in Sierra Leone and Guinea. The key shows what the colors mean.

In another instance, researchers in the United States tracked what people posted on Facebook and other social media about the flu. Looking at certain key words and where the people who posted them were located, the researchers predicted when and where a flu outbreak might occur.

Experts say the more sources of data they have and the better they can use computers to find health patterns, the easier it will be to stop the spread of some diseases.

From the basic sciences of chemistry to biology to the technology of the Web, from bioengineers making body parts to computer programmers detecting disease patterns, almost all area of medicine are constantly impacted by advancements in STEM fields.

 ## Text-Dependent Questions

1. What is one benefit in using computer models to predict if a new drug might produce side effects?

2. What makes up the human microbiome?

3. How did Atul Butte use Big Data to learn that a drug designed to treat depression might also treat lung cancer?

 ## Research Project

Do research online to find one kind of helpful microbe within humans.

Find Out More

Books

Kenney, Karen Latchana. *What Makes Medical Technology Safer?* Minneapolis: Lerner Publications, 2016.

Morrison, Heather S. *Inventors of Health and Medical Technology*. New York: Cavendish Square, 2016.

Websites

About Biomedical Engineering
www.embs.org/about-biomedical-engineering

The Center for Engineering in Medicine
cem.sbi.org/web/index.htm

IEEE Spectrum—Biomedical
spectrum.ieee.org/biomedical

Institute for Medical Engineering and Science
imes.mit.edu/

Science Daily—Health and Medicine News
www.sciencedaily.com/news/health_medicine/

Series Glossary of Key Terms

capacity   the amount of a substance that an object can hold or transport

consumption   the act of using a product, such as electricity

electrodes   a material, often metal, that carries electrical current into or out of a nonmetallic substance

evaporate   to change from a liquid to a gas

fossil fuels   a fuel in the earth that formed long ago from dead plants and animals

inorganic   describing materials that do not contain the element carbon

intermittently   not happening in a regular or reliable way

ion   an atom or molecule containing an uneven number of electrons and protons, giving a substance either a positive or negative charge

microorganism   a tiny living creature visible only under a microscope

nuclear   referring to the nucleus, or center, of an atom, or the energy that can be produced by splitting or joining together atoms

organic   describing materials or life forms that contain the element carbon; all living things on Earth are organic

piston   part of an engine that moves up and down in a tube; its motion causes other parts to move

prototype   the first model of a device used for testing; it serves as a design for future models or a finished product

radiation   a form of energy found in nature that, in large quantities, can be harmful to living things

reactor   a device used to carry out a controlled process that creates nuclear energy

sustainable   able to be used without being completely used up, such as sunlight as an energy source

turbines   an engine with large blades that turn as liquids or gases pass over them

utility   a company chosen by a local government to provide an essential product, such as electricity

Index

Credits

(Dreamstime.com: DT.) Addictivex/DT 7; Konovalovandrey/DT 8; Johannes Gerhardus Swanepoel/DT 11; Rebekah Flory/DT 12; Milovan Radmanovac/DT 13; Parys/DT 15; Dziurek/Shutterstock 17; Ali Riza Yildiz/DT 19; Niderlander/DT 20; Boris Ryaposov/DT 22; Olesia Bilkei/DT 24; Raysonho @ Open Grid Scheduler / Grid Engine 25; Clickandphoto/DT 26; Tyler Olson/DT 27; MIT 29; US Army 30; Peter Morenus/UConn Photo 33; Anyaivanova/DT 34; Andrewmits/DT 36; Science Pics/DT 38; Panagiotis Risvas/DT 40; Robert Semnic/DT 41; UC Davis Office of Research 42; bikeriderlondon/DT 44; Courtesy Nemours Children's Hospital, Orlando 45, 46, 47, 48; Crystal Craig/DT 48; Vvoevale/DT 50; Heiti Paves/DT 52; Pat Olson/DT 53; Evibeau/DT 55; Qiime.org 57; Monkey Business Images/DT 58; Centers for Disease Control 60.

About the Author

Michael Burgan has written more than 250 books for children and teens, many of them about science and technology. He has written biographies of Thomas Edison, George Washington Carver, and Nikola Tesla, among others, and explored such topics as making flu vaccinations, pursuing careers in genetic engineering and food science, and studying bats. A graduate of the University of Connecticut, Michael is also a playwright. He lives in Santa Fe, New Mexico, with his cat, Callie.